TSCHUDI, THE HARPSICHORD MAKER

Tschudi and his Family.

TSCHUDI
The Harpsichord Maker

BY

WILLIAM DALE, F.S.A.

MILFORD HOUSE
BOSTON

Library of Congress Cataloging in Publication Data

Dale, William.
    Tschudi, the harpsichord maker.

    Reprint of the 1913 ed. published by Constable,
London.
    1. Tschudi, Burckhardt, 1702-1773.   2. Harpsi-
chord.
ML424.T8D2 1973   786.2'3'0924 [B]   73-11229
    ISBN 0-87821-166-7

This Milford House Book is an unabridged
republication of the edition of 1913
Published in 1973 by MILFORD HOUSE INC.

Printed in the United States of America

TO

MISS LUCY BROADWOOD

THIS MEMOIR OF HER

DISTINGUISHED ANCESTOR

IS DEDICATED

WITH MUCH RESPECT AND GRATEFUL THANKS

PREFACE

THE object of the following memoir is to give in as brief a way as possible an account of the career of one of the distinguished London craftsmen of the eighteenth century, who, though a foreigner by birth, identified himself completely with the musical and social life of England, and obtained a reputation beyond the land of his adoption. The author claims no special fitness for the task save that the early years of his life were spent in the house in which Burkat Shudi lived and carried on his trade more than a hundred years earlier. At the time also of the compilation of Grove's *Dictionary of Music and Musicians* he was associated with the late A. J. Hipkins, F.S.A., in the preparation of some of the articles, and gathered together a good deal of the material supplied by that writer. To obtain this he made careful search for old business books of the eighteenth century in Shudi's house, and collected a mass of information, some of which is published for the first time in the following pages. The author also did much honorary work at the exhibition of Ancient Musical Instruments held at Albert Hall in connection with the Music and Inventions Exhibition of the year 1885. He arranged all the keyboard instruments, and wrote a descriptive catalogue of the same, receiving the award of a silver medal for his services.

He desires to acknowledge his deep indebtedness to Miss Lucy Broadwood, without whose valuable help the chapter on the early life of Burkat Shudi could not have been written.

CONTENTS

CHAPTER I

LIST OF ILLUSTRATIONS

CHAPTER I

THE HARPSICHORD DESCRIBED

FOR the sake of those who have but little acquaintance with the musical instruments of the past, it may be well to explain what the harpsichord was. The harpsichord was one of the immediate precursors of the pianoforte, and occupied an important position in the musical life of the eighteenth century. Like the virginal or spinet the sound was produced by a mechanical plectrum, which rose and plucked the string as each key was touched. The plectrum, which was of hard leather or crow-quill, was fixed in a contrivance called a jack, and when the jack fell after plucking the string a small piece of cloth inserted in it damped the sound. No expression was possible by means of the hand. To strike the key hard indeed produced less sound, a fact which is somewhat painfully evident in listening to those who play to-day

A

upon restored instruments of this family, and from mere habit act as if seated at a pianoforte. The touch required is more that of the organ. It is curious to note that as the harpsichord was being supplanted by the pianoforte, musicians were slow in learning the different technique demanded by the latter instrument. In the year 1799 a customer writes to Shudi's successor to have a Venetian swell put to a grand piano he has ordered. The Venetian swell was invented by Shudi for the harpsichord in 1769. The whole of the instrument was carefully closed in, and the top was covered with an arrangement like a Venetian blind, the shutters opening at a touch of the foot to let out the sound. Before putting the swell to the piano the maker writes : ' If the gentleman who wants the grand pianoforte is not positive in having a swell, we would thank you to persuade him off it, as it is a thing that adds much to the intricacy and weight of the instrument, and is of no advantage, the forte in the grand pianoforte being designed to be made with the finger and not with the foot like the harpsichord.' Nevertheless the swell was

2

put, but this protest was added: 'We hope you will not be offended with our declining to put a swell in future to any grand pianoforte, being convinced they deaden the tone to appearance, and being exceedingly troublesome to make, which, however, we should not mind did it answer to satisfaction.'

In the smaller contemporaneous instruments called spinets no expression at all was possible. By the spinet is meant an instrument roughly triangular in form, like a couched harp, which, as it cost much less, and was smaller than the harpsichord, was extremely popular from the time of the Restoration down to the end of the eighteenth century. The term virginal was also applied to these spinets. Indeed under the Tudors and up to the Commonwealth the word was used for any stringed keyboard instrument. Antiquaries now restrict it to the smaller coffer-shaped instrument, which is rarer than the spinet, much fewer having been made in England. So that the 'two pairs of virginals with 4 stops' mentioned in the privy purse expenses of Henry VIII. under the date of 1520

is interpreted to mean a double-keyed harpsichord in an outer case. By the 'pair of
excellent virginals' on which Prudence played
to Christiana in the house called Beautiful
John Bunyan probably meant a spinet. Samuel
Pepys also notices at the fire of London that the
'river was full of lighters and boats taking in
goods and good goods swimming in the water,
and only I observed that hardly one lighter or
boat in three that had the goods of a house but
there was a pair of virginals in it.'

The expression 'pair' means only a single
instrument, meaning perhaps gradation in the
old sense of the keys as steps through the
intervals of the scale. Some of these instruments were probably spinets. A most interesting notice of Pepys, under date 14th June 1661,
is : ' I sent to my house by my Lord's desire his
shippe and triangle Virginal.' Here we have
undoubtedly a true spinet, but the form being
new to Pepys he coins an expression for it, and
from its roughly triangular form calls it a
' triangle virginal.' His first use of the right
word is in 1668. ' To Whitehall, took Aldgate

4

Street on my way, and there called upon one Haward that makes Virginalls, and there did like of a little Espinette and will have him finish it for me, for I had a mind to a small Harpsicon, but this takes up less room, and will do my business as to finding out of chords, and I am very well pleased that I have found it.'

The great superiority of the harpsichord over these instruments arose from the fact that variety of tone could be produced by stops which controlled separate rows of jacks acting upon different strings. Technical descriptions of these stops, and the evidence concerning their invention, may be found in text-books. Suffice to say that the harpsichord in its most perfect form had the swell already described and four separate rows of jacks. By these one, two, or three strings could be plucked. One string, called the 'octave,' was below the others. It was tuned an octave higher, and was caught by the quill in the passage of the jack upward. Another pleasing variety of tone was the 'lute' stop. In this the strings were plucked closer to the bridge, producing a different set of

5

vibrations and a delicate reedy tone. The ' buff ' or ' harp ' stop effect was caused by small pads of leather pressed against each string and muting them. A stop at the left side could be worked by a pedal attached to the left leg, throwing on certain combinations without taking the hands from the keys. The two keyboards of the most expensive or ' double ' harpsichords enabled the various effects to be used in contrast. It has been the custom by some to depreciate the harpsichord and to pity those whose only keyed instrument it was. The tone has even been called a ' scratch with a sound at the end of it.' But such pity is certainly thrown away. The soft and delicate tones of the harp and lute stops, and the rushing crescendo of the swell, are effects which can only be heard on the harpsichord, and belong to the time when musical instruments were in their age of wood, and when metal did not rule. They are analogous sounds to the ' mildly pleasing strain ' of the ' warbling lute,' and the sweet moan of the recorder or *flute à bec.*

The harpsichord was largely used in public.

6

It was the constant support to the recitativo secco during the time of Handel and Bach. How well it served its purpose is strikingly illustrated by the fact that the earliest harpsichord of Shudi's known, made almost immediately after he began business on his own account, viz. in 1729, and which will be fully described later on, is still in use. Herr Paul de Wit, writing from Leipzig in November 1911, says : ' It has a most wonderful singing and carrying tone as one can realise, for it is regularly used to accompany the secco recitativo in *Don Giovanni* and *Figaro* in the big theatre that holds two thousand.' Also on the 17th April 1912 he further writes : ' The instrument is now at the Deutsches Theatre in Berlin, where it is used every evening for the representation of George Dandin by the Reinhardt ensemble. It has a wonderful tone, filling the whole room of the theatre.'

The last occasion on which the harpsichord was used in public, which the writer has been able to find, was at the rehearsal of the King's birthday ode at St. James's Palace on 4th June

1795. The King's band was a conservative institution, and would be likely to retain it as long as possible. Year by year a harpsichord was sent, so the books of Shudi and Broadwood record, for rehearsal and performance, but in 1795 a harpsichord was sent for the rehearsal and a grand piano for the performance. Always afterwards a grand piano is sent, ceasing in 1810.

The earliest pianos were of rectangular shape, afterwards called 'squares.' Although they rapidly found favour and quickly displaced the spinet, it was really the grand piano which effaced the harpsichord. Where the piano was for a long while is shown by an entry on 12th May 1781, when Clementi left London for a series of concerts, beginning at Paris. 'A harpsichord and a pianoforte shipped to Paris for Mr. Clementi.' The harpsichord was undoubtedly the solo instrument, and the piano must have been a small square, for the term 'grand' does not come into use before 1790, and the few that were made previous to this were always called 'large pianofortes.' Clementi's

8

piano was sent to be used for accompaniment only, as in 1767, when at the performance of the *Beggar's Opera* at Covent Garden, Mr. Dibdin accompanied Miss Brickler 'on a new instrument call'd pianoforte.'

When we turn to the use of the harpsichord in private, we can only conclude that its employment was very limited. Here our compassion is not wasted. The great length and tenuity of the strings kept it constantly out of tune, and the octave string made matters worse. Tuning contracts were by the quarter. A guinea was paid, and although the number of visits is not stated they were probably not less than six. Even this was not enough for some. On 7th April 1772 ' Mr. Ward paid his bill and agread to have his Harp^d. tuned every week for 2s. 6d., the 7th being the first time.' £6, 10s. a year for tuning, bearing in mind the relative value of money, was a good round sum to pay, in addition to which was constant requilling and regulating. Only a small part of each crow-quill was of service, and the consumption of them must have been enormous. One firm

orders ' 8000 crow-quills at 10s. 6d. per 1000.'
The full length of a double harpsichord was
8 ft. 10 in., and the cost with Venetian swell was
85 guineas, at the time when the annual rental
of the mansion at Hyde Park Corner, where
St. George's Hospital now stands, was £60 per
annum. Evidence as to the actual number of
harpsichords made is given by the fact that
Burkat Shudi and his son numbered their
harpsichords consecutively, and we learn from
this that during the whole of their career they
did not make more than twelve hundred.
Yet their successors from 1782 to 1802 made
no less than seven thousand square pianos and
over a thousand grands. The lifelong com-
petitors of the Shudis, the Kirchmanns, may
have made more harpsichords, but as they did
not number them we have no means of telling.
The story told by Burney in Rees's *Cyclopedia*
of the distress of Jacob Kirchmann at the ladies
forsaking the harpsichord for the guitar is
amusing. He says : ' The vogue of the guitar
was so great among all ranks of people as
nearly to break all the harpsichord and spinet-

makers, and indeed the harpsichord masters themselves. All the ladies disposed of their harpsichords at auctions for one-third of their price, or exchanged them for guitars, till old Kirchmann, the harpsichord-maker, after almost ruining himself with buying in his instruments for better times, purchased likewise some cheap guitars and made a present of several to girls in milliners' shops, and to ballad-singers in the streets, whom he had taught to accompany themselves with a few chords and triplets, which soon made the ladies ashamed of their frivolous and vulgar taste and return to the harpsichord.'

It would not be fair to close this brief account of the English harpsichord without saying a word concerning the singularly beautiful grand piano which replaced it, an instrument as unlike a modern grand as can well be imagined. The writer possesses one of 1793 made by Shudi's son-in-law, John Broadwood, which is numbered 521, and is exactly similar to the instrument Joseph Haydn must have played upon in 1792 at his own and Madame Mara's concerts at

Saloman's Rooms.   The grands of this period
were made exactly on the lines of the harpsichord, supported on a frame, and with the pedal
feet projecting from each front leg.   The curve of
the bent side was even more elegant than that
of the harpsichord.   The hammers were covered
with hard and thin wash leather to produce a
harpsichord tone.   The loud pedal lifted the
dampers from the strings as now.   Each note
had three strings, those in the bass being thick
brass wire only, and it was possible by means of
the soft pedal to shift the hammers not only on
to two strings, as in modern grands, but also
on to one only, which is not possible now.   This
is the *una corda*, a sign found in the writings
of old composers, which has now become
meaningless.   The sympathetic vibration of the
untouched strings produced a beautiful effect.

The rapid spread of the pianoforte and the
increasing demand for it even in the closing
years of the eighteenth century is remarkable.
America at this time was becoming a great
market for pianos, and the orders sent by one
John Bradford of Charleston, South Carolina,

GRAND PIANOFORTE OF 1793 BY JOHN BROADWOOD

during these years are quite a revelation. It was the custom for clients to write in the order-book, which Shudi's son-in-law kept, their wishes, and to this circumstance we owe the preservation of the following autograph entry, which is copied verbatim. The tragic interest lately attached to the name is sufficient excuse for quoting it.

' 14 *March* 1795.

' GENTLEMEN,—Please to make me one of the best Grant Pianofortes you Can. I Rely on your Honor to let it be a good one. I wh to have it Plain in every Respect and the case of handsome wood, the Pelly may be screwed fast. When Done call on Mr. George Astor for the payment. I shall wish to have it ship^d in July or August by the ship Hope for New York or any other good ship.—I am, Gentlemen, With Respect, Yours,   JOHN JACOB ASTOR.

' CITY COFFEE HOUSE,
  ' CHEAPSIDE.'

CHAPTER II

BURCKHARDT TSCHUDI or, as he afterwards
anglicised his name, Burkat Shudi, was born at
Schwanden in the canton of Glarus in Switzerland on the 13th March 1702. It is scarcely
possible to find a fairer valley in all Switzerland
than that in which Schwanden is situated,
surrounded as it is by snow-clad peaks and
watered by two rushing torrents, the Sernf and
the Linth. The locality is out of the beaten
track of tourists, and quite unknown to them.
The people to-day are described as extremely
diligent, honest, and unspoilt, educated to
citizenship from boyhood. Burckhardt's father,
Joshua, was a wool-merchant, a councillor, and
a surgeon. The house in which he was born
still stands, but is broken up into tenements, and
is a tinware factory. His mother was an Elmer,
a name which later on in 1735 figures among the

14

SCHWANDEN, GLARUS

wadding-makers. Thanks to the extreme care with which the death-rolls, church-books, and other archives of Glarus are kept it is possible to trace the Tschudis back through many centuries. Much information concerning them was published in the *Jahrbuch des Historischen Vereins des Glarus* in 1899. A native of Glarus and connection of the Tschudis, Professor Blumer, compiled a genealogical tree, which he carries back to Johann, Mayor of Glarus, born about 870, and establishes that Heinrich, born 1074, died 1149, made Feodary of Glarus by Lady Gutta, Abbess of Seckingen, was the first to adopt the name of Schudi (*sic*). It would be outside the scope of this memoir to dwell upon the ancestry of Burckhardt Tschudi, or to describe the important offices held by members of the family, and the high position they always had in their lovely native valley. Their character was of the sternest and most uncompromising mould. Industry, skilfulness, and the power to succeed and excel, even when fortune frowned, seem always to have been characteristics of the Tschudis, and to have come as naturally to them as the free mountain air they breathed. Their place in Europe no doubt nurtured these qualities. A living descendant of Tschudi's writes : ' His uncompromising disposition was a race characteristic, bred of the many centuries' long struggle against Austria's encroachments, and the severe climate of Glarus. Through all their history, carefully chronicled like that of other leading Swiss families, can be traced the Tschudi dogged determination to overcome difficulties and maintain their independence. This Swiss spirit impressed even Buonaparte, so that when under the convention he was dividing up Europe he neutralised their federation and granted a continuation of local self-government to Glarus and the adjoining cantons. Also the Tschudis never forgot that their origin was as old and noble as the Hapsburgs whom they withstood.'

Young Burckhardt was taught the trade of the joiner, and must have begun early, for he left his native valley, never to return, at the age of sixteen. He was taught the trade by his uncle, also a Joshua, who is described as

'Schreinermeister Leutnant und Schützen-meister im grossen Mühlehaus in Schwanden.' It would probably be more correct to call the trade he learnt cabinet-making. Glarus, especially Schwanden, provided slates in wooden frames for almost the whole of Europe, and also made wooden cabinets and tables with fine polished slate tops, and other slate articles which were exported everywhere. These slate tables, beautifully framed in wood, were made largely for inns, and are still to be found in use. Slates for writing purposes formed also one of the joinery industries of Schwanden. In addition, there was a large exportation of the more beautiful woods in the seventeenth century. The age of oak for furniture was passing away, and walnut, cherry, hornbeam, and pine are particularised, in addition to which finely-cut wood for musical instruments is mentioned, this being called 'Geigenspelten' (fiddle-boards). This was probably the wood of the spruce-fir (*abies excelsa*), chosen for its lightness and resonance to-day as the sounding-board wood for the modern piano. The violin-makers of

Cremona may have drawn their wood from Schwanden, and the great Antwerp harpsichord-makers of the seventeenth century most likely did the same.

But the early years of the eighteenth century brought bad times to Schwanden. The wood in Glarus began to run short. The slate workers in many cases turned wood-merchants, and travelled to distant parts for their finer woods, which they cut up where they found it and sent it to England. In the second decade of the century the deforestation had become so serious that the Cantonal Parliament resolved that for ten years in no community or parish might wood be sold outside the country. It is also recorded that 'Timber trade is not so flourishing as in former times. Maser-holz is not so easy to find, and the English have imported from Canada a wood that is better liked. Also the prevailing fashion of panelled cupboards and whole rooms (using walnut) has decayed.'

The distress was great, and the joiners or cabinet-makers suffered most. It is no small

tribute to the courage and indomitable persever-
ance of the Glarus folk to add that foreseeing
greater misery in store they turned their talents
to cotton-weaving. One of the first to set up
a loom was Burckhardt Tschudi's father. The
loom grew to many until the trade was so
important that up to a hundred years ago
Glarus sent cotton goods all over the world.
Competition has robbed this industry of some
of its importance, but to this day quantities
of ' Oriental ' patterned goods still go from
Schwanden to the East.

It is not hard, after all that has been said, to
understand why the young joiner, Burckhardt
Tschudi, decided to leave his much-loved native
valley and seek his living elsewhere. What it
cost him to do so can well be imagined. But
there was a special reason for his choosing
London. The church - books of Schwanden
contain entries concerning another well-known
Glarus family, the Wilds, who were directly
descended from Anna, sister of the reformer
Zwingli. Amongst them are the following :
' Church-elder, Joh. Wild, 1694-1756, dwelt

many years in London, succeeded in his profession, and made a very good fortune,' also 'Merchant Hans Jakob Wild, 1674-1741, lived many years in London and died in the house of his son-in-law, the clavier-maker, Burckhardt Tschudi.' Further particulars of their callings are not given, but it is fair to assume they were among those who left Schwanden in the early days of the distress and in advance of Burckhardt. Jakob Wild's wife was Salome Kubli, and it was their daughter Catherine, born 1704, that Burckhardt married. It is not known when Jakob Wild left Schwanden. It may not have been very long before Burckhardt's departure. He indeed and Catherine perhaps played together as children in the Glarus valley, and the thought of meeting her again may have made his migration less hard to bear. Though Burckhardt did not return to Schwanden he did not forget it, nor was he forgotten. The Glarus *Zeitung* says : ' His native village honoured him by choosing him as Father of the Church, though he always lived in London. He acquired a large fortune, but more than this was the

20

faithful love and honour he paid his parents, for whom he provided in their declining years.' It is not clear if this refers to Burckhardt's own parents or to Jakob and Salome Wild. Probably both are meant. The last-named certainly died in Tschudi's house in London.

Arrived in London young Tschudi obtained work in the house of one Tabel, a Flemish harpsichord-maker working in London in Swallow Street, St. James's. It was, naturally, in such a business that his skill in fine joinery work would be best employed. His nephew, later on, in an advertisement he sent forth, says : ' Harpsichord makers must be joiners and is the coffion course of our business.' Concerning this Tabel scarcely anything is known. It is Dr. Burney who tells us Tschudi went to him, and James Tschudi. Broadwood, writing in 1838, gives us the important information that Tabel had learned his business in the house of the successor of the Ruckers of Antwerp. He also adds that Tabel, it is believed, was the first person who made harpsichords in London. This latter statement can hardly be true. Pepys, recording his visit in 1666 to the spinet-maker Haward, says he had 'a mind to a small harpsicon,' which looks very much as if Haward were making them at this time. There is besides a harpsichord by John Hitchcock, also a spinet-maker, at the South Kensington Museum, and although Hitchcock's date is not known it can hardly have been later than the closing years of the seventeenth century. But that there was very little harpsichord-making in England before the days of the great manufacturers, Tschudi and Kirchmann, is certain. Though known here in the sixteenth century the instrument was imported from Italy, the land of its birth, and in the next century almost entirely from Antwerp. From 1579 and onwards for about one hundred years there flourished at Antwerp four generations of harpsichord-makers of the famous family of the Ruckers. No other instruments ever approached theirs for their sweet silvery tone and beauty of workmanship as well as durability. They were quite unlike the English instruments. The cases were usually japanned.

22

The sounding-board was ornamented with a
rose-hole and painted with flowers, while the
rest of the interior was decorated with a lovely
shade of red. Often the lid was painted inside
by some master painter, or else inscribed with
mottoes. One by Andries Ruckers, the elder,
dated 1614, has a painting by Van der Meulen
within the top. One purchased by the private
secretary of Charles I. for that monarch by
Hans Ruckers, the younger, was painted inside
by Rubens, the subject being Cupid and Psyche.
Owing to the high artistic character of their work
the Ruckers belonged to the Guild of St. Luke,
the Painters' Guild. The last of the Ruckers
passed away long before the seventeenth century
had closed. Yet their instruments remained in
use for more than a century after and were
highly prized. As late as 1770 one fetched the
enormous price, at that time, of £120, and as late
as 1820 one Preston, a music-dealer in the Strand,
had one made by Hans Ruckers, the elder, which
was bought at the demolition of Nonsuch Palace,
and was said to have been Queen Elizabeth's.
When the outer case decayed, or grew shabby,

and the keys were worn through, it was the custom to have them entirely recased in mahogany, ornamented with stringing, according to the fashion of the time. New keys were put and little was retained save the interior bracing, and the precious sounding-board on which their marvellous tone depended. As late as 1772 Tschudi had two Ruckers harpsichords in constant use, and his books contain such entries as these : ' Mr. Lee had the Ruker for one night.' ' Miss Fleming hired the little Ruker.' ' Duchess of Richmond had a new double harpsichord instead of a Ruker for hire.' ' Lady Pembroke hired the little Ruker for Brighthampstone.' ' Lady Cathren Murray hired the little Ruker harpsichord.' These instruments must have been considerably more than one hundred years old at the date of the entries. Over sixty Ruckers harpsichords are in existence at the present time.

Who succeeded the Ruckers is not known.

Probably the great Antwerp manufacture ceased before the end of the century, and Tabel, with whom we are more intimately concerned, somewhere about 1700 settled in London. It is recorded in 1777 that 'Lady Howe bought a second-hand harpsichord by Table' (*sic*), a solitary instance of the mention of the name. Fortunately there is one specimen of his handiwork in existence, in possession of Helen, Countess of Radnor. A glance at it shows from whom he learned his business. His name is inscribed, just as Andries Ruckers did, in Roman capitals three quarters of an inch long: 'Hermanus Tabel, Fecit, Londini 1721.' There is a rose-hole in the sounding-board. The naturals are black, and the sharps veneered with a slip of ivory at top. The stops are two on each side, lute and octave, and first and second unison. The cabinet-work is excellent, and in it young Tschudi may have had a hand. Tabel lived till 1738, and his will was proved early the following year. He mentions a brother in Amsterdam and his wife, to whom, after a few pecuniary bequests, he bequeaths the residue of his estate.

Not only was Tschudi employed by Tabel but also his competitor Kirchmann. Burney calls them Tabel's foremen, but he is far from accurate, for he says Kirchmann did not come to London till 1740, which was two years after Tabel's death. He must have been some time previous to this in Tabel's employ, seeing that, according to the same authority, he succeeded to the business and married the widow. The story as told in Rees's *Cyclopedia* runs as follows : ' Kirchmann worked with the celebrated Tabel as his foreman and finisher till the time of his death. Soon after which, by a curious kind of courtship, Kirchmann married his master's widow, by which prudent measure he became possessed of all Tabel's seasoned wood, tools, and stock-in-trade. Kirchmann himself used to relate the singular manner in which he gained the widow, which was not by a regular siege but by storm. He told her one fine morning at breakfast that he was determined to be married that day before twelve o'clock. Mrs. Tabel, in great surprise, asked him to whom he was going to be married, and why so soon ? The finisher told her that he had not yet determined whom he should marry, and that if she

26

would have him he would give her the preference. The lady wondered at his precipitancy,
hesitated full half an hour, but he, continuing
to swear that the business must be done before
twelve o'clock that day, at length she sur-
rendered; and as this abridged courtship pre-
ceded the marriage act, and the nuptials could
be performed at the Fleet or May Fair without loss of time or hindrance to business, the
canonical hour was saved, and two fond hearts
were in one united in the most summary way
possible just one month after the decease of
Tabel.'

Kirchmann did not continue Tabel's business,
but set up independently in Broad Street, and
in his harpsichords retained the rose-hole in the
sounding-board, which Tschudi did not. He
adopted as his sign the King's Arms. The King
and the Prince of Wales were notoriously un-
friendly, and as Tschudi adopted for his sign
the Plume of Feathers we note in these signs the
difference of patronage. It was long supposed
that Tschudi commenced business for himself
in Great Pulteney Street, and the traditional

date is 1732. It cannot have been so, for his
earliest harpsichord known is dated 1729, and
it certainly was not the first. Nor did he begin
in Pulteney Street but in Meard Street. It is
a striking testimony to the ability of this
Schwanden joiner that probably by the time
he was twenty-five he had become a skilled
harpsichord-maker, and was working on his own
account. The fine early eighteenth-century
houses on the south side of Meard Street still
retain much of their ancient respectability,
and lest they should ere long take their place
among vanishing London a photograph has
been taken of them. In one of these houses
Tschudi began his career of prosperity. Here
it was that Handel so often came, and it was not
till Jakob Wild, his father-in-law, had died in
1741 that he removed. The *Daily Advertiser*
of 5th October 1742 contains the following
advertisement: 'This is to give notice that
Burkat Shudi, Harpsichord-maker to his Royal
Highness the Prince of Wales, is removed from
Meard St. in Dean St., Soho, to Great Pulteney
St., Golden Square.'

MEARD STREET, SOHO

Tschudi's Early Life

The house in Great Pulteney Street has been rebuilt within the last few years. That in Meard Street still stands, although the exact house is not known.

CHAPTER III

TSCHUDI AND HANDEL

In mentioning the removal of Tschudi from Meard Street to Great Pulteney Street we anticipate events and must return. Tschudi's marriage to Catherine Wild was an important time in his life. Unfortunately the date of the marriage is not known, and careful search for it in the registers of St. James's and St. Anne's has not been successful. It has been fixed as early as 1728 and as late as 1732. Somewhere between those dates it took place. If the earlier date it would agree very well with the time of his quitting Tabel, and commencing for himself the manufacture of harpsichords. It is also not certain if he began in Meard Street. The probability is strong that he did; and if doubt is entertained that a young man of some twenty-five or twenty-six years should be able to take a good house in a respectable quarter, it must be

Handel
by Mercier.
(By permission of the Earl of Malmesbury.)

borne in mind that Jakob and Salome Wild were prosperous people, and Tschudi's marriage with Catherine may have brought the means to start him on his successful career. The Wilds lived in Meard Street with Tschudi, as we have seen, and it was not till Jakob had died in 1741 that Tschudi removed. The end house which faces Dean Street is dated 1732, but the rest of the street may be a few years earlier.

The most important factor in Tschudi's success was his friendship with Handel. According to Tschudi's grandson, Handel was a constant guest at his table, which was ever well covered with German dishes and German wines. How this friendship came about is not clear. It began before Tschudi had gained any great repute at his trade. There must have been quite a Swiss circle at Soho when Handel came to London for the second time in 1718. We read in the chronicles of Schwanden of Hans B. Zopfi, 'Claviercordmacher,' who died in London in 1750, of whom absolutely nothing is known; of a picture-frame-maker, Stahelin,

31

dying also in London in 1739; and in 1753 Samuel Blumer, member of another well-known Glarus family, calls himself 'late foreman to Mr. Shudi.' For three years Handel was chapelmaster to the Duke of Chandos and lived at Cannons. In the year 1729 he entered into partnership with Heidegger of the King's Theatre, and in the same year set out for Italy for singers for his new operas. Amongst those he brought back was Anna Strada del Pò, who was the only one who remained faithful to him, and did not desert him for the rival new opera in Lincoln's Inn in 1733. Burney calls her a coarse singer with a fine voice. She had so little to recommend her to the eye that she was nicknamed 'the pig,' and it took her some time to get into favour. Handel took pains with her, wrote for her, and advised her, and at length rendered her equal to the first singers of the Continent. She did more to make Handel a national favourite than any other singers, though he had the pick of them. On 31st March 1730 a benefit was given for Anna Strada, attended by His Majesty, when *Julius Cæsar* was the opera.

HARPSICHORD MADE FOR ANNA STRADA

Throughout that year she grew steadily in powers and favour as a singer. She left finally in 1738.

Some six or seven years ago Herr Paul de Wit of Leipzig purchased in Rome a fine double harpsichord, which has already been referred to in the opening chapter, bearing the inscription: 'Burckat Tschudi, Londini, fecit 1729.' It is in every respect a replica of the only Tabel harpsichord known. The name is in Roman capitals three quarters of an inch long in Ruckers' style. The 'furniture,' *i.e.* the brasswork of the stops, hinges, catches, etc., is Tabel's, and the keyboards are the same, the naturals being black and the sharps veneered atop with ivory. The stops also are four, lute and octave, and first and second unison. As an early work of Tschudi's, showing clearly that he was hardly emancipated from the atelier of Tabel, this instrument would be interesting, but there is more about it than this. On removing the name-board the following inscription is seen at the back: 'Questo cimbalo è dela Sig^ra Anna Strada 1731, London.'

Here, undoubtedly, is an instrument made by
Tschudi in 1729, and becoming the property of
Anna Strada in 1731. Who but Handel could
have given it to her ? To this very instrument
she must have sung, and on it Handel must have
accompanied her. The date associated with
Strada's name is the year when she had gained
popularity. One pictures Handel in Meard
Street choosing it or superintending its manufacture, and it probably figured in her benefit
at the King's Theatre.

The mention of a harpsichord so authentically
connected with Handel leads us to the con-
sideration of the vexed question of the harpsichords which are said to have been his. Handel
bequeathed to his amanuensis, Christopher
Smith, all his MSS.; and Smith, out of gratitude
to the King for the pension allowed him after
Handel's death, gave them to George III. With
the MSS. Handel also left Smith his ' large '
harpsichord, which Smith in turn is said to have
given to the King with the MSS. There are two
claimants to the honour of being the harpsichord
which became Smith's. The first is an Andries

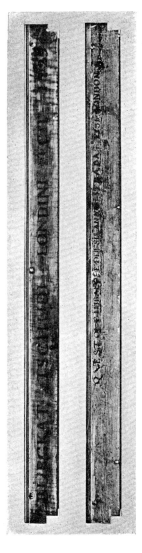

NAME BOARD OF HARPSICHORD MADE FOR ANNA STRADA (FRONT AND BACK)

Ruckers, dated 1651, and now in the South Kensington Museum, where the testimony concerning it is also deposited. It is in the original japanned case, and the interior of the lid is inscribed with mottoes. In the year 1883, however, there was discovered in Windsor Castle a wrecked harpsichord of Joannes Ruckers, dated 1612, which was brought to the notice of Mr. W. G. Cusins (afterwards Sir William Cusins). In arranging and cataloguing the Loan Exhibition of Ancient Instruments at Albert Hall in 1885 this harpsichord passed through the writer's hands, and at his suggestion sets of keys were made for it to improve its appearance. The original case and keyboards were gone, and but little remained except the sounding-board and name. Having been found at Windsor Castle it was exhibited with a notice that it 'may have been the large harpsichord mentioned in Handel's will bequeathed to Christopher Smith and given by him to the King.' At the present time it is on loan at the Victoria and Albert Museum, with a label attached that it was ' bequeathed by Handel to

35

George II.' The statement in the *Times* that the ' keys, jacks, and stops are of modern make ' is not correct. Jacks and stops (the knobs only are gone) are original. The date of the double keyboard has already been mentioned. To any one familiar with the terms used in the eighteenth century neither of these instruments answer to the description ' large harpsichord.' The English harpsichords of this time were from eight to nine feet long, and the Ruckers harpsichords, averaging some seven feet, were called ' little.' It is far more probable that it was a Shudi which has now been lost sight of, though Handel may in addition have had a Ruckers, seeing that Shudi had them in stock. The discussion may be closed in the words of one of the greatest musicologists of the Victorian age, the late Carl Engel. Speaking of a little clavichord in the Town Museum of Maidstone, said to have belonged to Handel, Engel writes in the *Musical Times* for August 1879 : ' If I were to give a list of all the musical instruments said to have belonged to Handel, which have been brought under my notice, I should probably

36

surprise the reader. Not only would it include organs, fiddles, and harpsichords, but even various tuning-forks, and the very anvil of the famous Harmonious Blacksmith. Indeed, no other list of this kind which I might compile would surpass it in comprehensiveness, unless it be a list of the harps and guitars said to have belonged to Queen Marie Antoinette.'

The finest portrait of Handel in existence is that by Philip Mercier, in possession of the Earl of Malmesbury. Mercier was a German painter of French extraction, and came to England from Hanover with Frederick, Prince of Wales, the son of George II. and father of George III., whose portrait he painted and brought with him. Handel's portrait has on the back of the canvas the following inscription : 'Portrait of Mr. Handel given by him to Thomas Harris, Esquire, about 1748.' It was probably painted a little earlier, at the time when he had recovered from his bankruptcy of 1745, and when his health and his fortunes had taken a turn for the better; for we read in

the *Letters of the First Earl of Malmesbury* that
Lord Shaftesbury reports him in 1746 as never
looking so cool and well, and says that he had
been buying some fine pictures. Thomas Harris
was the brother of James Harris, who became
first Earl of Malmesbury. The more gifted of
the two undoubtedly was the elder brother
James, known in the brilliant literary circle in
which he moved as ' Hermes ' ; but Thomas was
equally fond of music, and it is evident was
among those who formed the inner circle of
Handel's friends. It is ' Councillor ' Thomas
Harris who witnessed Handel's will and the
first three codicils. In the last codicil he
becomes a beneficiary by a legacy of £300.
In the picture the composer is seen hard at
work, his wig laid aside and his shirt un-
buttoned, while his harpsichord is open at his
side. Through the kindness of the present
Earl of Malmesbury the picture is here for the
first time faithfully reproduced with its acces-
sories. The harpsichord, evidently painted from
one at which Handel actually sat, is extremely
interesting. It is not a Ruckers but an English

instrument of the least expensive make. It is
'single,' that is, having only one row of keys,
and as only one stop is shown on the left-hand
side, there could have been only three in all—
octave, first unison, and second unison. But
the keyboard is the most noticeable. The
black sharps are inlaid with a white slip, which
was the custom of both John and Thomas
Hitchcock, and was imitated by several other
English makers. That Shudi occasionally
adopted this form of keyboard is known, for
the two harpsichords of 1766 by him, so long
preserved in the apartments of Frederick the
Great in the New Palace at Potsdam and now
in the Hohenzollern Museum at the Palace of
Monbijou in Berlin, have such keyboards.
The harpsichord therefore shown in the Mercier
portrait may well have been one of Shudi's.
Several of Handel's MSS. accompanied the gift
of the picture to Thomas Harris and are preserved at Heron Court.

We have reverted to the anglicised form of
writing Shudi's name, because it was his custom
so to inscribe his instruments after the time of the

Strada harpsichord, with the single exception
of the two just mentioned which went to
Frederick the Great. Yet his calligraphy was
always German, as will be seen by the autograph
here reproduced, which was found underneath
the sounding-board of a harpsichord of 1761.
One result of Handel's connection with Shudi
was his introduction to Frederick, Prince of
Wales, which entitled him to use the crest of
the Plume of Feathers as the sign of his house
when he removed to Great Pulteney Street.
To it we also owe the preservation of another
early harpsichord made for the Prince in 1740
and sent to Kew Palace. It is now at Windsor
Castle, and was exhibited at the Loan Collection
at Albert Hall in 1885. It is a double harpsichord, not large in size, and has the lute stop.
On the first key Shudi wrote: ' No. 94, f. 1740.'
The number gives us some idea of Shudi's
trade. He had now been making twelve years,
and this works out at an average of about
eight a year. In the height of his career he
never made more than sixteen or eighteen
per annum. It was not long after the date

40

TSCHUDI'S AUTOGRAPH

of the Prince of Wales's harpsichord that Shudi, owing no doubt to increased patronage, removed to the wider and more fashionable street close by named after Queen Anne's Prime Minister.

CHAPTER IV

SHUDI AND FREDERICK THE GREAT

NOT very long after Shudi's establishment in
Pulteney Street was painted the picture of
himself and family, which is fairly well known
through forming the frontispiece to Dr. Rim-
bault's *History of the Pianoforte*, although the
reproduction there given does not do justice
to the excellence of the painting. Shudi is
engaged in tuning a harpsichord, which is placed
on a richly gilt stand, and is evidently something
out of the way. He wears a flowing dressing-
gown. His wife, Catherine Wild, takes her
tea, and the two young boys stand near. The
attire of all the family and their surroundings
betokens a prosperous man. It was painted so
as to fill a space in the panelling over the fireplace in the little front parlour of Shudi's house
in Pulteney Street, and there it remained until
some fifty years ago. Unfortunately the name

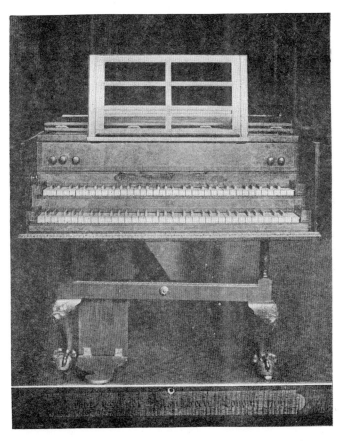

HARPSICHORD MADE FOR FREDERICK THE GREAT.   No. 511

HARPSICHORD MADE FOR FREDERICK THE GREAT. No. 511

of the painter is not known, and speculation has been rife. It was attributed by Sir John Millais to Zoffany, on account of its conversational style, but it does not resemble Zoffany's work. It was exhibited in 1892 at the Winter Exhibition at Burlington House. The *Times* critic, after speaking in its praise, says : ' It is curious that the record of the painter's name should be lost. Certainly Hogarth did not paint it, and it is so much finer in execution than the conversation pieces of his English contemporaries, that we are inclined to look abroad among Shudi's foreign countrymen for the artist. The drawing and modelling are admirable— but in the colouring there is something crude and hard, which recalls the German work of the period.' Remembering the intimate connection between Philip Mercier and both Handel and the Prince of Wales, as well as Shudi's relations with both, one naturally looks to this painter as the author of the picture. Unluckily Mercier's work is rare and scattered, and although the authorities at the National Portrait Gallery dismiss him from the reckoning their judgment can by no means be considered as final. It certainly does not resemble the small Watteau-like group of Frederick, Prince of Wales, and the three princesses, painted in 1733, which is in that gallery. But at a later period Mercier had a bolder and larger style, to which the Shudi picture belongs. Its resemblance to the portrait of Handel just described is very striking. Both pictures are of the same period, and are far removed from Mercier's earlier French manner. It would seem as if Mercier adopted this style when he lost the favour of the Prince of Wales and was dismissed his service.

The picture was painted about 1744. This is gathered from the age of the two boys. The elder, Joshua, was eight and the younger, Burkat, a year or two younger. According to a family tradition the harpsichord Shudi is tuning is one of which he made a present to Frederick the Great on the occasion of his winning the battle of Prague, which was fought in the above year. Shudi was a stout supporter of the Protestant cause in Germany, and the King of

44

HARPSICHORD MADE FOR FREDERICK THE GREAT. No. 512

Shudi and Frederick the Great

Prussia was then supposed to be fighting its battles. Evidence of Shudi's connection with the great Frederick is given by the fact that he possessed a ring which was given to him by that monarch, bearing his portrait. It is mentioned in Shudi's will, and he bequeaths it to his friend and compatriot the organ-builder Snetzler. This highly-prized ring cannot now be found. There is no trace of any harpsichord in Germany so early as the date referred to. If one went, it could hardly have been lost sight of, remembering the great care with which all the possessions of Frederick were preserved. It is also strange that in 1766 not one, but two, fine double harpsichords specially made should have been sent him, which were preserved with other heirlooms and memorabilia of Potsdam in the rooms where they were first placed, up to within the last few years. The late A. J. Hipkins got over the difficulty by suggesting that the two last-named harpsichords were a royal commission which was given to Shudi to execute as the result of his gift some twenty years earlier, and he believed in the ' battle of Prague ' harpsichord being sent, though he could find no trace of it. Such documentary evidence as we have speaks of one harpsichord only, and gives the date as 1765. Thus, the Swiss lexicon, published at Zurich in 1795, says: 'From the Schwanden branch also descended Burckhardt, a poor journeyman cabinet-maker, who came to England, and became famous at the Court in London as a harpsichord-maker. Among other beautiful things, he made for the King of Prussia in 1765 an elegant harpsichord, with two manuals. Burckhardt Tschudi married in London, where he died in 1773.'

Again the *Allgemeine Augsburger Zeitung* of 1765 says: 'The celebrated Klaviermacher, Burckhardt Tschudi, a born Swiss of Schwanden in the canton Glarus, had the honour to make a harpsichord with two keyboards for His Majesty the King of Prussia, which was very much admired by all who saw it. It was remarked as an extraordinary thing that Tschudi has placed all the registers in one pedal, so that they can be taken off one after the other, and the decreasing and increasing of the tone can be produced at

HINGES OF ONE OF THE HARPSICHORDS MADE FOR
FREDERICK THE GREAT

will, which crescendo and decrescendo harpsi-chord-players have long wished for.'

This description may be taken to mean the control of the side or machine stop by the foot, and the crescendo and decrescendo referred to the Venetian swell which was applied to the Potsdam harpsichords of 1766, though the patent for this invention was not taken out till 1769. The article further goes on to mention that 'Tschudi was proud to have his royal harpsichord played upon for the first time by the most celebrated player of the world, the nine-year-old music-master Wolfgang Mozart.' The contrivances which are said to have been so much admired were new to Germany, and a great advance on the capabilities of the instruments in use in that country at the time.

It is to be noted that both these accounts refer to one harpsichord only. They, however, can only be based on the two harpsichords of 1766, which may have been made early that year, or possibly dated a little in advance. It is curious that the writer on applying to a friend in Berlin for the latest information concerning these instruments, which he was unaware had been removed from Potsdam, received the following reply: 'I am informed that a Tschudi harpsichord of the year 1766 from one of the Royal Castles is now at the Hohenzollern Museum in Berlin. It is the harpsichord which I believe was presented by Tschudi to King Frederick the Great after the peace with Austria.'

Owing to the kindness of Dr. Seidel, the director of the Hohenzollern Museum, photographs have been taken of the two harpsichords in question. Both were made and sent together, for they are consecutive numbers, 511 and 512. The pattern of the 'furniture' of both is the same. The keyboards are of the beautiful Hitchcock style, the sharps being inlaid with a slip of ivory. They have the full number of stops—machine, lute, octave, buff, first unison and second unison, and the Venetian swell was applied. Full directions for the working of these stops are given on No. 511, showing how novel the improvements were.

Shudi's books of this time are not in existence, nor does there appear to be any record

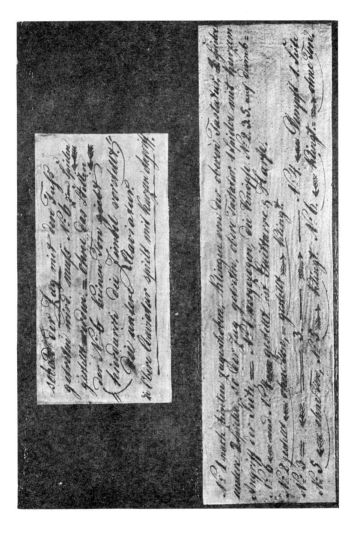

DIRECTIONS FOR USE OF THE STOPS ON ONE OF THE HARPSICHORDS MADE FOR FREDERICK THE GREAT

at Berlin of their coming into the country. Here, however, are two fine and carefully constructed harpsichords made by Shudi in the zenith of his career, made certainly for Frederick the Great, when he had nearly completed the *Neues Palais* at Potsdam, and according to Burney placed the one in the apartments of his sister the Princess Amelia and the other in that of his brother Prince Henry. Burney describes only the first one, No. 511, on oxidised silver legs. Both are inscribed 'Burckhardt Tschudi, fecit, Londini, 1766,' though he had long since called himself Shudi, and both may now be seen together in the Hohenzollern Museum.

CHAPTER V

SHUDI AND HIS APPRENTICES

OF those who helped Shudi in his business there is but little known. Burney is our informant that Johann Zumpe was one of his men. If so it must have been not much later than the middle of the eighteenth century, for in the early sixties of that century Zumpe had commenced making the small clavichord-like table pianos, which rapidly became popular, attracting to this country for their manufacture quite a number of other Germans, such as Schoene, Ganer, Pohlmann, Beck, Buntebart, Garcka, Beyer, Froeschley, etc., traditionally known as the twelve apostles, although more than that number could be enumerated, many of whose instruments are known, bearing dates from 1766 to 1780 and later. There is a bill-head existing of one Samuel Blumer, who calls himself 'late foreman to Mr. Shudi.' The date is given on

TSCHUDI'S HOUSE IN GREAT PULTENEY STREET, SOHO

the back of the bill-head, which is a receipt for
£63, paid by Madam Alt for an upright harpsichord on 22nd August 1753. At the top of the
bill-head is an engraving, which represents
Blumer engaged in tuning a harpsichord while
a lady and gentleman stand near. The whole
is an evident *réchauffé* of the picture of the
Shudi family group. Blumer styles himself
' Harpsichord and spinet maker in Great Poult-
eney Street, West Golden Square, London.'
It is curious he should have established himself
in the same street as his master, but their
relations were probably friendly. Blumer is
the name of an old Schwanden family still
living in that valley, and Samuel doubtless was
one of the joiners who were driven from home
by the distress, and found work and help through
the kindness of his fellow-countryman.

Better known than Blumer was Shudi's
nephew Joshua, between whom and his uncle
relations became very strained. Joshua came
from a quarrelsome stock. He was the son of
Nicholas Tschudi, Burckhardt's elder brother,
born in 1700, a serjeant-major of cavalry. On

the 15th March 1742 Nicholas Tschudi and Jakob Hefti, a butcher, of Schwanden, fought together in the public-house of Rudolf Knecht. Neither were wounded severely, but one Hans Brauer, a dealer in cattle, who tried to separate them, paid for his intervention with his life, and died two hours after. Nicholas fled to England and came to his brother Burckhardt, who naturally did not welcome him very cordially. Subsequently he went to Holland and finally emigrated to America, where he died on 10th January 1760. Condemned for his crime to a lifelong exile he never saw Schwanden after leaving it. His son Joshua was born in 1739. He may have been brought by his father to Burckhardt as a young child, together with his sister Anna Margarett, who afterwards married Zopfi, the harpsichord-maker mentioned in chap. III. It is known that Burckhardt dealt kindly with Joshua, and apprenticed him to the joinery trade, afterwards taking him into his house as a harpsichord-maker. How Joshua repaid this kindness is revealed by several advertisements in the *Gazeteer* of 1767. Joshua

left his uncle's employment and set up business
for himself in the street at the end of that in
which Shudi lived, viz. Silver Street, Golden
Square, and adopted as his sign the Golden
Guitar; whereupon Burckhardt advertises that
he has no connection with Joshua, and throws a
slight upon his work by saying that he was only
a joiner, which, though excusable under the
circumstances, it must be owned was a little
unreasonable, seeing how his own career began.
Burckhardt also prides himself upon the fact
that his 'mistery' had never been communicated to any one. Joshua's advertisement in
reply is as follows :

' GAZETEER.

' *Jan. 12th*, 1767.

' Joshua Shudi, harpsichord maker, having
offered his services to the nobility and gentry in
a manner which he thought could not give the
least offence to his uncle, to whom he has been
a faithfull servant, and in quitting his service
had an undoubted right to make use of his
abilities for the support of himself and his
family, finds himself attacked in a most un-

53

generous manner, and expressions made use of which have not the least foundation in truth. He is sorry to expose any one, but is compelled to speak of facts. His uncle did put him apprentice in the manner he describes, but he forgot to mention that he himself was brought up in the same manner. Harpsichord makers must be joiners, and is the comon course of our business. I wish he had joined a little more truth to his assertions, and then he would have said that after my long service, my steady application to business, and my care of his interest in every respect would have induced him to have kept his promise of taking me into partnership as a reward, which his own conscience must tell him I deserved, if he has any conscience at all. What I assert I am ready to give convincing proof of to any lady or gentleman who will do me the honour to apply to me at my apartments at the Golden Guitar, in Silver Street, Golden Square. I have now by me harpsichords of my own making, which I shall be glad the best judges will make trial of, and desire no more favour than merit deserves.

54

Harpsichords repaired or finished, and as to tuning, even my uncle allows me capable. If he never comunicated his mistery, as he calls it, to any one, what figure will his apprentices make.'

The use of the word 'mistery' by Burckhardt is interesting, and Joshua evidently does not quite understand it. The late A. J. Hipkins thought that the word was used in the sense of something occult or mysterious, and suggested that the secret which Burckhardt had never communicated was the art of tuning in equal temperament, the getting rid of the 'wolf' at the end of the scale. This was already known and practised at the time, for Emanuel Bach expressed his preference for it. But the old method of tuning was carried on in pianos as late as 1846, and so long as Dr. Buck was organist, the organ in Norwich Cathedral was so tuned. Burckhardt, it will be noticed, correctly spells the word 'mistery.' In indentures the word came to be spelt 'mystery' by confusion with the word with a different meaning. He means nothing more than his 'mistere' or 'métier,' his art and craft. So used the word had already become archaic, and Joshua apparently does not quite see its application.

Joshua Shudi died in 1774, and a year after, in the *Public Advertiser* for 16th January 1775, is another advertisement :

' HARPSICHORDS.

' Mary Shudi, of Berwick Street, St. James', widow of Joshua Shudi, nephew and disciple of the late celebrated Burkat Shudi, harpsichord maker, takes the liberty to inform the nobility, gentry, etc., that she has now by her, ready to be disposed of on reasonable terms, a great variety of exceeding fine toned single and double harpsichords. To be seen and tried at her house as above. N.B.—Mary Shudi solicits the continuance of those favours the indulgent public were pleased to confer on her late husband ; and begs leave to assure them that any order they may be pleased to honour her with shall be pleasingly and carefully executed.

56

HARPSICHORD BY SHUDI AND BROADWOOD OF 1770

Shudi and his Apprentices

Instruments tuned in the most exact manner on the shortest notice. A genteel first floor to lett, with other conveniences.'

The only harpsichord of Joshua Shudi's known is dated 1776. The widow, therefore, must have continued to use his name.

One reads between the lines of Joshua's advertisement the sting of his remarks levelled at his uncle's apprentices, and the cause of his leaving Pulteney Street. Shudi had two sons, the elder of whom, Joshua, died in 1754 at the early age of eighteen. Burkat, the remaining son, was brought up in the business and carried on the name after his father's death, until the harpsichord had ceased to be used. Not long before the death of Joshua, the son of Burckhardt, there came to the house a young Scotsman, born at Cockburnspath, who, as his countrymen are wont, came to London to seek his fortune. He was a cabinet-maker just out of his time, and if report be true walked to London with the proverbial half-crown in his pocket. However this may be he was a young

57

man of genius and ability, who quickly rose in his trade, and obtained the prize which the nephew missed—a partnership with the elder Shudi, afterwards continued with Burkat the son. He further fulfilled the conditions of an industrious apprentice by gaining the affections of Shudi's only daughter Barbara, to whom he was married in 1769. The same year was taken out the patent for the Venetian swell already referred to, ' so much admired by all lovers of Musick,' and not long after was made the fine double harpsichord in the writer's possession which is inscribed: ' Burkat Shudi et Johannes Broadwood, Londini, fecerunt 1770. No. 625.' It was made for Dr. David Hartley, after whom Hartley Coleridge was named, and was rescued from a stable near Newbury in 1881. Strangely enough a harpsichord made the following year, No. 639, bears the name of Burkat Shudi only.

At her marriage Barbara, according to the custom of the time, started a housekeeping book. The entries in it belong principally to the short seven years of married life, and are mostly memoranda of personal matters mixed

HARPSICHORD BY SHUDI AND BROADWOOD OF 1770

up with some business details, showing a curious mingling of trade and home life, which reads strangely in our days. Barbara died in 1776, and the entries which are hers are the sole mementoes we have of this only daughter of Shudi and Catherine Wild. For this reason a few of them are worth quoting. The book begins with a list of clothes and housekeeping accounts of all sorts: A wax doll costs 2s. 6d., a pair of shoes 3s. 8d., and a silk ' petecoate ' £1, 3s. The various commodities she bought were ' ryce, suggr, oyle, sellet, grins, fishe, sellery, catshep, etc.' Pork and veal were 5d. a lb., and so was backon ; tea, 10s. and 12s. a lb. She makes a memorandum that her father has given her a ten-pound note, and then puts down ' Lady Campbell, Lady Manners, Duk of Argile,' which are orders for harpsichord-tuning.

It appears also to have been her duty to record the various means of transport, and so she writes: ' The Atherston waggon setts out from the Castle and Falcon, Aldergate Street, every Wednesday morning early. The Stafford waggon at do. every Tuesday morning. St.

Neots wagg., Three Cups, Aldergate Street, every Saturday at 12 o'clock M. Northampton waggon, Windmill, St. John Street, Monday, W. F. (Wednesday, Friday), and Saturday, at 12 o'clock. Daventry and Northampton waggon, the George, Smithfield, W., Sat. 3. The Northampton waggon setts out from the Ram, Smithfield, Tuesday, and arives at Northampton on the Friday following, and setts out again on Friday and arives at Northampton Tuesday. The Stamford Hunts waggon goes from the Castle and Falcon, Aldergate Street, on Tuesday and Saturday morning at 10 o'clock, and from the White Harte, St. John's Street, on Tuesday, the goods to be taken the night before. Bungay, Suffolk, setts out from the Saracen's Head, Snow Hill, on Saturday evenings. Worcester waggon setts out from the Bull and Mouth, Bull and Mouth Street, by Smith., on Tuesday evening.'

The entries about her servants are fairly frequent : ' Ann Watson came to my service 13th February, 1769, agreed £5 wages and tea.' Later comes ' July 13th, agreed for to raise Ann

Watson's wages to £6 per ann., and a guinea for tea and a half a crown per quarter for shoes.' 'June 12th, 1771, Ann Watson for 6 months' wages due last April 13th, £3, do. for tea 10s. 6d., for cleaning of shoes, 5s.' 'February 12th, 1772, Ann Davis came to my service, agreed £6 wages and her tea.' 'Ann Gibbard came to my service, agreed £8, and to find herself tea, a month's wages or a month's warning.' This is the first time that this occurs. The following October we find: 'received a quarter's wages, due September 18th, £2.' Ann Gibbard appears to have left on May 3rd, 1773, for we find 'recd. contents in full and all demands for 8 months' wages, £5,' and the signature 'Ann Gibbard.'

Finally we have the record concerning Margaret Panzetta, who stayed from 1774 until after her mistress's death: 'Dec. 29th, 1774, Margaret Panzetta came to my service, agreed for the first year £6, 10s. and to find herself tea.' On the 21st January 1775 she is paid one guinea and two muslin handkerchiefs which are put down at 7s. Then follows: 'received for one year and a quarter's wages 18 Nov. 1776 the sum of £7, 18s. by me, Margarett Panzetta.' The final entry is: 'received on the 17th Feb. 1777 of John Broadwood the sum of £10, 6s. due to me for 11 months' servitude, Margaretta Matilda Panzetta.'

The book continues for a time after Barbara's death, and becomes increasingly a record of items paid. The small square pianos which had then become popular were carried home by a porter on his back, and the payments for such service are frequent.

CHAPTER VI

SHUDI AND HIS PATRONS

IT is not difficult to realise the life that Shudi led in Pulteney Street in the times of prosperity that set in at his removal there, which continued to his death in 1773, and were afterwards enjoyed by his son. But we must dismiss from our minds modern ideas concerning business, and rest assured that no social stigma was attached to the fact that Shudi was, after all, only a craftsman, nay, even a mechanic, who lived at his shop. Everything indicates that he mingled on equal terms with the famous people of his day. Handel was but the beginning of a number of musicians who sought his house and were welcome at his table. On taking one of Shudi's harpsichords to pieces it was found that the visiting-cards of those who had called at the 'Plume of Feathers' had been used up to fill vacant spaces in the regulation where needed. The uncompromising, independent manner which was his hereditary gift followed him through life. It is said that he never made a harpsichord so long as he had one unsold, some colour to which is given by an entry on 21st January 1773: 'Dutches of Malbury bespoke a harpsichord.' There was no need for him to seek custom. It came as thick and fast as he could deal with it. No other serious competitor was in the field save Kirchmann, whose instruments were of a different calibre, and drew their own patrons. This restriction of his business was awkward sometimes. An entry, 'Burkat's harpsichord sent on hire to Miss Chumley,' shows there was no available instrument in the showroom, not even 'the Rooker' or the 'little Ruker,' and so young Burkat's own harpsichord had to be sent from one of the private rooms.

The 'Plume of Feathers' was an ordinary four-storied house in a then fashionable street. Here the manufacture was carried on, new instruments were sold or old ones repaired, and in the midst of it all Shudi and his family led their domestic life, which was one of refinement and comparative ease. The front door, furnished with a ponderous knocker of the Queen Anne type, was kept closed. Immediately to the right as one entered was a little parlour with panelled walls. Over the fireplace were two recesses in the panelling, one of which contained a bevelled mirror in carved frame, and the other the much valued picture of Shudi tuning the harpsichord surrounded by his family. There was, of course, a grander room than this, where the group was posed by the painter. It will be noticed in the painting that three pictures hung on the wall behind the harpsichord. Two of these are portraits of Frederick, Prince of Wales, and the Princess Augusta. The middle picture, which is a landscape, is supposed to be a representation of Shudi's native valley in Glarus, but all these pictures are now no longer traceable. The showroom was probably the room on the left of the doorway. There was also most likely some extension of the premises at the back, where the much despised but necessary ' joinery ' was done. In the top lofts of the house the writer himself discovered a store of crow-quills, carefully tied up in bundles, which must have lain there for some hundred years or so. The sweet tinkling sound of the harpsichord, being tuned constantly, filled the house. The phonetic spelling that is always used in the books recalls to us the speech of those who lived then. Such words to wit as 'pattant,' 'consort,' 'reharsle,' 'qarter,' 'Malbury,' etc., all and many such which were pronounced as they were written.

Any attempt at regular book-keeping does not begin before Barbara's marriage in 1769. Earlier books may have contained so much private matter that Shudi's descendants destroyed them. The extracts given, therefore, must be considered to belong to the closing years of the elder Shudi and to the years of the partnership of young Burkat with John Broadwood. The last royal commission executed by Shudi was a fine double harpsichord made for the Empress Maria Theresa in 1773, numbered 691. This instrument, fortunately, like the Prince of Wales's and Frederick the Great's harpsichord,

66

is still in existence. It was obtained by Mr. Victor Mahillon in Vienna, and is now in the Conservatoire Royal at Brussels. The entry of its departure is made on 20th August 1773, the day after Shudi died, and reads simply: ' Sent the Emperess' Harpsichord on board ship '; so prominent a figure in Europe need only to be described as ' The Empress.' Two years later, and probably as the result of this order, another harpsichord was sent to Vienna for Joseph Haydn, which is numbered 762, and is still preserved in that city as a valued relic of the great musician to whom it belonged. After Haydn's death it was Herbeck's, and is now in the Musickverein at Vienna.

While being thankful that so many Shudi harpsichords remain to us, there are some that have quite disappeared, which we would give much to have with us. Perhaps none more so than the one referred to in an entry which reads as follows :

' 1774, March 5. Mr. Dashwood and Gardine bought a harpsichord, No. 708, for Mr. Gainsborough, painter in the Circle Bath.

67

' March 11. Mr. Gainsborough's harpsichord was packed and sent to Bath.'

' Mr. Gardine ' is, of course, Felice de Giardini, the famous Italian violinist, at this time leader of the Pantheon Concerts, and doubtless a frequent visitor at Pulteney Street. His friendship with Gainsborough, who painted his portrait, is well known, as well as the musical tastes of the painter himself. It is too much to hope that No. 708 has escaped destruction. As pianos came into use harpsichords were ruthlessly destroyed, and so completely has their memory passed away that modern writers take no pains to ascertain what instruments were used in the eighteenth century but call them all pianos. Gainsborough's harpsichord is a case in point. The above entry was discovered by the writer in 1881, and was communicated correctly to several in the literary world at that time. Yet Mrs. Arthur Bell, in her *Life of Gainsborough*, simply says that he ' bought a piano in 1774 '; and writing further, concerning Fischer's portrait, says that he is ' seated at a piano,' of which Gainsborough gives the maker's name

68

'Merlin.' This Merlin was a harpsichord-maker
of the time, several of whose instruments still
exist.

Gainsborough's rival, Sir Joshua Reynolds,
was also a constant customer, particularly of
the younger Shudi. He does not appear to
have ever purchased a harpsichord, and probably
would not require one continually. There are,
however, several entries of harpsichords sent
to him upon hire, no doubt for the use of the
literary and artistic friends who met at his
house. No address is given. Indeed very few
London addresses of customers are quoted, it
being understood that everybody knew where
they lived.

On 7th January 1776 'Mr. Moreland's new
harpsichord was sent to Bedford Street. The
number of the harpsichord 758.' This may have
been the father of George Morland. In 1793,
the year young Shudi ceased to make harpsichords, there is another record in connection
with the artistic world: 'Taking a harpsichord
to Mr. Bartolozzi, 207 Piccadilly (a print shop).'

The charge for the hire of a harpsichord was

10s. 6d. per month. On the 25th November 1771 we read : 'Lord Sandwich sent for a double harpsichord,' and on the 3rd December, 'Lord Sandwich sent ye harpsichord home,' employing his own conveyance. Harpsichord-tuning varied according to distance and perhaps according to the social position of the customer. Thus on 31st July 1772 'Miss Naville at Ipsom' pays 5s., but the 'Princess Amelia at Gunnessbury' pays £1, 1s. 'Miss Seoan of Rigate,' 10s. 6d., while 'Lady Chesterfield by ye Qarter' pays £1, 1s. for probably six or eight visits. On the 4th June 1773 the 'Prushian Embasander' pays 4s. for the tuning of a 'pianoforte,' which must have been a small square by a German maker.

After the death of the elder Shudi it was still not easy to obtain a new harpsichord, for on 6th June 1774 'Mr. Robt. Palmer bespoke a harpsichord with a swell.' To enumerate all the nobility whose names occur in the books of this time would be a lengthy task. A few culled at random are the Duke of Queensberry, the Duke of Devonshire, the 'Dutchess' of

Norfolk, the Earl of Sandwich, Earl of Plymouth, 'Dutchess of Ritchmond,' Lady Stoverdale, and Lady Pembroke. Some, such as 'Lady Giddion' and Lady Archer, have harpsichords 'for a consort.' The entries are mostly that of the name, only meaning tunings. Sometimes weeks pass without a sale. Lady Stoverdale of Redlinch, near Bruton in Somerset, purchased on 10th August 1775 a double harpsichord numbered 750, which it is hoped is still in existence, as it was for sale in a shop at the West End of London some twelve years ago. Occasionally one meets with a harpsichord in a special case. On 24th December 1774 'Miss Skeine bought a octava harpsichord, Blew bordered, No. 710.' Also the last harpsichord made at Pulteney Street in March 1793 for Mr. Henry de la Maine of Cork is described as a 'Double keyed harpsichord with swell, etc., cross banded with sattin wood. Cypher in front, etc. £84.'

The account of the Earl of Hopetoun contains an item of twenty-five guineas for eight and a half years' interest on an unpaid bill.

The entry that the ' Dutchess of Ritchmond '
had a ' new double harpsichord for hire instead of
the Ruker ' reminds us of the ultimate fate of
the two Ruckers harpsichords so long used by
Shudi as hack instruments.   Neither of them
fetched the good prices these instruments were
supposed to command.   But the grand piano
had now become the rage, and the days of the
harpsichord were over.   Their last appearance
is thus recorded :

' 12th March 1790.   Lord Camden for two
harpsichords, the one a Ruker, double row, the
other a Kirchmann, octava, 25 gs. each.'

' 12th July 1792.   Mr. Williams for a double
keyed Rucker harpsichord, £26, 5s.'

The crowd of musicians whose names appear
in the books in the two last decades of the
eighteenth century belong properly to the early
days of the grand pianoforte.   They include
every name of any importance, but it would be
outside the scope of this work to dwell upon
them.   One of the most frequently quoted
names is that of Dussek, for whom in 1794 the
first grand pianoforte with six octaves is made.

Joseph Haydn also is lodged in the same street at No. 18, nearly opposite. In the harpsichord days, however, professional engagements figure largely. Witness the following entries :

' 20 Feb. 1772. A Reharsle of yᵉ Oritorio.

' 5 March 1772. Sold Mr. Hullmandel a harpsichord made by Scouler for 25 Guineas.

' 26 Feb. 1773. Sent Lord Grovenors harpsichord to Mr. Arnold's Oritorio.

' March 3, 1773. Oritorio Drurie Lane.
Oritorio Arnold.'

(This was probably Dr. Arnold's Oratorio of the Prodigal Son produced this year.)

' 6 March 1773. Oritorio.

' 7 Thacht house.

' 9 A Reharsle.

' 13 Oritorio.

' 14 Thacht house.

' 16 A Reharsle.'

These entries indicate that for the frequent performances of oratorios and for the concerts at the Thatched House, which was the recognised concert-room previous to the opening of the Hanover Square rooms, harpsichords remained permanently, and were only tuned for the various occasions. The rehearsals which are entered separately probably took place at Pulteney Street, and are noted only for the purpose of charging the tuning.

Young Clementi, it will be remembered, took a Shudi harpsichord with him to Paris, and also one of the small square pianos which were now being made in such numbers. As the result of this visit the following order was executed:

' 23 Oct. 1784. Pascall Taskian.

' 4 Pianos, one plain, 3 inlaid without stands, shipped to Paris.'

Taskin of Paris was the famous harpsichord-maker to Marie Antoinette.

It remains only to subjoin a list of the harpsichords by Shudi and Shudi and Broadwood known still to exist. Additions to the list would be gladly welcomed.

Number.	Date.	Number.	Date.
—	1729	750	1775
144	—	762	1775
229	1749	789	1776
260	1751	862	1779

74

Shudi and his Patrons

Number.	Date.	Number.	Date.
407	1760	899	1781
427	1761	902	1781
511⎫ 512⎭	1766	919	1782
625	1770	955	1789
639	1771	1137	1790
686	1773	1148	1791
691	1773	1155	1793

CHAPTER VII

THE PIANO OF DON MANUEL DE GODOY

IT is somewhat inexplicable that the art of painting was never in England allied with harpsichord-making. Even Tabel, direct from the house of Ruckers, made his instruments plain, and so did Kirchmann and Shudi, although the latter put fine cabinet-work in the exterior, especially about the middle of the eighteenth century, when the age of walnut was being merged into the age of mahogany. A judicious combination by him of both woods had a charming effect. The large strap hinges of the top used by both makers were also very striking. But the writer cannot find a single instance of a harpsichord that was painted or decorated after the manner of the Flemish makers. With the early days of the grand piano, however, the fashion came in of decorating the exterior of the case with Wedgwood medallions, and

76

GRAND PIANOFORTE MADE IN 1796 FOR DON MANUEL DE GODOY

in the year 1796 there was made by Shudi's
son-in-law an instrument with this decoration,
upon which no pains or cost were spared. Its
historic interest and singular beauty, as well
as the fact that it is still in existence, is sufficient
excuse for closing this notice of Shudi's career
with a brief description of one of the most
costly instruments of the kind ever made in
his house. This grand piano, of harpsichord
shape, was made for Don Manuel de Godoy,
the handsome guardsman, the favourite of
Queen Maria Louisa, whom Charles IV. of Spain
raised to the rank of Minister of Foreign Affairs.
The year before the order for this piano was
given, Godoy earned the title of Prince of the
Peace by concluding the Treaty of Basle with
the French republic, and two months after the
piano reached the shores of Spain he signed the
Treaty of San Ildefonso and declared war with
England, initiating that series of disasters for
his country which culminated at Trafalgar.
It is most probable that Godoy was in London
himself in the spring of 1796, for one of the
decorations named is ' The Prince's portrait in

front by Taylor, £10, 10s.' Alexander Taylor, the miniaturist, was an occasional exhibitor at the Royal Academy for twenty years, the last time he exhibited being in 1796. The price paid for the portrait is a high one, and Godoy no doubt sat for it. The piano was not for himself, however. Sheraton's own design for the instrument, of which more than one copy has been preserved, states it was presented by Godoy to the Queen of Spain.

The order was taken on the 8th February 1796, and is thus entered:

' Prince of the Peace,

      Le Comte de Mopox el de Jarnico,

Grenier's Hotel, Jermyn St.

recommended by Mr. Christian, 22 College Hill, a G.P.F. add. keys C in basse to C in alt. in sattinwood case superbly ornamented with inlaid work and Wedgwood's and Tassie's medallions, etc.'

It took four months to make, and was shipped on 22nd June 1796, and is thus described as

' Mopox,

        ' A G.P.F. add[1]. keys from C to C in

sattinwood case superbly ornamented. A cover of green striped leather and stockings for the legs. A Green baize Cover and two quires of silver paper in two very strong deal cases, the frame in one and case in yᵉ other marked C.D.S.C. No. 1 and 2. Delivered at the Bull, Porters Galley Key for the Esperanza, Belotte, Bilbao.'

The cost is fully set out as follows :

The Count Mopox Grenier's Hotel. Dr.—

A Grand Pianoforte 6 octaves C to C, in sattinwood case ornamented with different woods with water gilt mouldings and Wedgwood's and Tassie's medallions, etc., The Prince of Peace's arms chased and gilt in burnished gold rich carved frame, etc. — £223 13 0

The Prince's portrait in front by Taylor — 10 10 0

A Cover of green striped Leather and stockings for the legs . . . — 9 9 0

A Green baize Cover . . . — 1 7 0

A Deal case very stout for the Instr. . — 5 10 0

A do. do. frame . — 5 7 0

Strings, forks, etc. . . . . — 1 1 0

Cartage to the Key . . . . — 0 7 6

£257 4 6

Tschudi, the Harpsichord Maker

Sheraton's design for this instrument was preserved by the maker, but concerning the piano itself nothing was known until a few years ago, when a Parisian dealer in antiquities wrote to a lady in England, whom he knew to be a collector of things rare and curious, that he had a grand piano in satin and other woods made by John Broadwood in 1796 and covered with medallions. It was none other than Don Manuel de Godoy's present to the Queen of Spain, and it is now in a London drawing-room. Probably looted from Spain in the Napoleonic wars it remained unknown but well cared for during a number of years, most likely in some French chateau, until thrown upon the market and purchased by this Parisian dealer. It is in splendid preservation. The satinwood has mellowed with age, the keys are unworn, and the medallions perfect. As it stands it is a good illustration of the warfare between the designer, who wants to be artistic, and the manufacturer, who must obey the requirements of a musical instrument. Sheraton designed separate and unconnected legs for the piano.

80

It was at a time when such a thing was not known, but the maker appears to have given in and abolished the frame and stretcher, although in the particulars concerning the packing he still speaks of the supports as 'the frame.' Sheraton did not make any provision for the pedals. These, had the older fashion been adhered to, should have been made to project from each front leg of the frame. They were made to depend from the body of the piano, and a third pedal added in the middle, perhaps in Spain, acts upon a pad which presses against the sounding-board, producing a sourdine effect. This arrangement spoils the general effect of the lower part, and was never contemplated in the original design. 'The Prince's portrait in front by Taylor,' alas, is no longer there, and its fate, needless to say, is not known! Perhaps Queen Maria Louisa removed it. Above the keyboard, surrounded by beautiful decorated work, is an oval, where it was usual to engross the maker's name and date. In this case the unusual course has been taken of inscribing the name on the rail covering the dampers. The oval is now filled with a device, somewhat clumsily put on, which occupies the place where once was Taylor's miniature of the Prince of the Peace.

Through the kindness of the owner a representation of this beautiful instrument is given. The compass of six octaves was then thought to be the last word, but it has gone on increasing; and owing to its increase and the heavier construction and greater size which more modern tastes demanded, the beautiful form and proportions of the harpsichord and harpsichord-shaped pianos have gone for ever.